EXPLORING
A COMPREHENSIVE
BY
WILLIAM JONES
2023

Exploring Ghana: A Comprehensive Travel Guide by William Jones
This book edition was created and published by Mamba Press
©MambaPress 2023. All Rights Reserved.

Contents

Preface: Unveiling Ghana's Tapestry
    Introduction: Ghana - A Tapestry of Timeless Beauty
    Chapter 1: Discovering Accra - The Capital City
    Chapter 2: The Cape Coast and Elmina - A Journey through History
    Chapter 3: Kumasi - The Cultural Hub
    Chapter 4: Wildlife Wonders - Mole National Park
    Chapter 5: Kakum National Park - Canopy Walk and Beyond
    Chapter 6: The Volta Region - Serenity by the Lake
    Chapter 7: Beyond Borders - Togo and Côte d'Ivoire
    Chapter 8: Ghanaian Cuisine - A Gastronomic Odyssey
    Chapter 9: Festivals and Celebrations
    Chapter 10: Ghana's Artistic Tapestry
    Chapter 11: Coastal Charms - Exploring Ghana's Hidden Beaches
    Chapter 12: Practical Travel Tips
    Epilogue: A Journey Unveiled
    Appendix: Additional Resources

Preface
Unveiling Ghana's Tapestry

Welcome, fellow travelers, to the enchanting realm of Ghana, where the cadence of history harmonizes with the pulsating rhythms of daily life. As you embark on this literary journey through the pages of our travel guide, envisage the verdant landscapes, feel the warmth of the Ghanaian sun on your skin, and immerse yourself in the kaleidoscope of cultures that define this West African gem.

Ghana, perched on the Gulf of Guinea, is a nation that transcends the boundaries of time, a repository of stories etched into the very fabric of its being. It beckons those who seek to unravel the layers of its history, to bask in the glow of its diverse traditions, and to witness the resilience of a nation that has overcome the trials of time.

In the following pages, we invite you to traverse the length and breadth of this captivating country, from the bustling streets of Accra to the serene shores of the Volta Lake. Each step you take unveils a chapter of Ghana's narrative, a story that resonates with echoes of ancient civilizations, colonial struggles, and the triumphant emergence of a proud, independent nation.

This travel guide is not a mere compendium of facts and figures; it is a portal through which you will be transported into the very soul of Ghana. Together, we will navigate the vibrant markets of Accra, where the ebb and flow of commerce are a testament to the city's dynamic spirit. We will stand in awe before the historic forts and castles along the coast, where the haunting whispers of the trans-Atlantic slave trade still linger.

As we journey to Kumasi, the cultural heart of the Ashanti Kingdom, and wander through the sprawling markets of Kejetia, let the vibrancy of Ashanti traditions envelop you. Venture into the untamed wilderness of Mole National Park, where the trumpeting calls of elephants echo through the savannah, and traverse the treetop canopy walkway of Kakum National Park, suspended in nature's embrace.

The Volta Region, with its tranquil lakes and cascading waterfalls, awaits exploration, offering respite from the bustle of urban life. Cross borders into Togo and Côte d'Ivoire, discovering the interconnected tapestry of West African cultures that transcend geopolitical boundaries.

No exploration of Ghana would be complete without savoring its culinary delights. From the aromatic spices of jollof rice to the hearty flavors of waakye, Ghanaian cuisine reflects the nation's history, blending indigenous ingredients with influences from across the globe.

Our journey extends beyond the physical landscapes, delving into the rich tapestry of Ghanaian festivals and celebrations. From the lively parades of the Aboakyere Festival to the spiritual significance of the Homowo Festival, each celebration is a testament to the resilience, creativity, and communal spirit that define Ghana.

In the final chapters, practical travel tips serve as your compass, guiding you through the intricacies of planning a seamless journey. From visa requirements to health considerations, we aim to empower you with the knowledge needed to navigate Ghana with ease and confidence.

As you turn the pages of this guide, envision yourself not merely as a tourist but as a participant in a cultural odyssey. Let the words be your guide, the stories your companions, and Ghana itself your host. For every traveler, this is an invitation to not just witness but to engage, to embrace the richness of a nation that invites you not as an outsider, but as a guest in its home.

So, let the exploration begin. Unveil Ghana's tapestry, one chapter at a time, and may your journey be as enriching and captivating as the nation itself.

Introduction
Ghana - A Tapestry of Timeless Beauty

In the heart of West Africa, where the warm embrace of the Gulf of Guinea meets the undulating landscapes of a nation steeped in history, Ghana unfolds as a tapestry of timeless beauty. This introduction serves as your gateway to a country whose essence transcends the boundaries of conventional travel. Ghana is more than a destination; it is an odyssey through the epochs, a journey through the annals of civilization, and an immersion into the vibrant cultures that have shaped this West African gem.

A Geographical Overture

Ghana, situated on the west coast of Africa, is a nation of contrasts and cohesion. Bordered by Côte d'Ivoire to the west, Burkina Faso to the north, Togo to the east, and the Atlantic Ocean to the south, its geographical diversity mirrors the complexity of its cultural mosaic. From the tropical rainforests of the south to the savannahs of the north, Ghana's landscapes offer a kaleidoscope of ecosystems, each contributing to the country's unique allure.

The coastal plains, dotted with palm-fringed beaches and bustling fishing villages, give way to the lush vegetation of the central regions. Moving northward, the terrain transforms into the savannahs of the Ashanti and Northern Regions, home to diverse wildlife and traditional farming communities. Alongside these geographical wonders, the Volta Lake, one of the largest artificial lakes in the world, punctuates the landscape, reflecting both the nation's commitment to progress and the resilience of its people.

A Symphony of Cultures

Ghana is a nation that echoes with the harmonies of cultural diversity. With over 100 ethnic groups, each preserving its unique traditions and languages, Ghana is a testament to the celebration of differences within a collective national identity. The Akan people, predominantly in the central and southern regions, contribute significantly to the cultural tapestry, with the Ashanti and Fante subgroups particularly influential.

In the north, the Mole-Dagbon people, the Gonja, and the Mamprusi, among others, infuse the region with their distinctive traditions. The Ewe people, residing in the Volta Region, contribute a rich heritage of music, dance, and spirituality. The Ga-Dangme people, indigenous to the Greater Accra Region, are the custodians of the vibrant capital city, Accra.

The interplay of cultures is not confined to the borders of Ghana alone. The nation shares cultural affinities with neighboring countries, fostering a sense of regional unity. This interconnectedness is evident in shared traditions, languages, and historical narratives, making Ghana a microcosm of West Africa's cultural dynamism.

Historical Resilience

Ghana's history is an intricate mosaic, each piece contributing to the nation's resilience and progress. The region known as present-day Ghana has been inhabited for millennia, with evidence of ancient civilizations such as the Akwamu, Akan, and Ashanti kingdoms. However, it was the emergence of the trans-Atlantic slave trade that etched a dark chapter in Ghana's history.

The coastal forts and castles, notably those at Cape Coast and Elmina, stand as solemn witnesses to the horrors of the slave trade. Yet, these monuments also symbolize Ghana's ability to overcome adversity, as the nation emerged from this dark period to champion the cause of freedom and independence.

In 1957, Ghana became the first sub-Saharan African nation to gain independence from colonial rule, setting the stage for the decolonization of the continent. The leadership of Kwame Nkrumah, Ghana's first president, played a pivotal role in not only securing independence but also in advocating for the unification of African nations. Ghana's commitment to Pan-Africanism remains

Chapter 1
Discovering Accra - The Capital City

In the rhythmic heartbeat of Ghana, Accra stands as the pulsating epicenter. The capital city, a kaleidoscope of tradition and modernity, invites travelers to unravel its layers, explore its dynamic streets, and immerse themselves in the vibrant tapestry that defines this urban gem.

A City in Motion

Accra, situated along the Gulf of Guinea, is a city that defies stagnation. Its streets are alive with the constant ebb and flow of life. From the energetic markets to the bustling neighborhoods, Accra's dynamic spirit is palpable. The city, once a hub of the trans-Atlantic slave trade, has metamorphosed into a symbol of resilience, progress, and cultural richness.

As you navigate the streets of Accra, the contrasting elements of the old and the new coalesce seamlessly. Colonial-era architecture, reminiscent of the city's past, shares space with contemporary structures, creating a visual narrative that mirrors the city's evolution. Independence Arch, standing proudly at the Black Star Square, is a testament to Ghana's journey to sovereignty, while the towering skyscrapers in the business district speak of a nation on the rise.

Markets and Merchants

To truly understand Accra is to venture into its markets, where the heartbeat of the city reverberates. Makola Market, a bustling hive of activity, is a sensory symphony. The vibrant colors of textiles, the heady aroma of spices, and the rhythmic banter of traders create an immersive experience. Makola is not merely a market; it is a microcosm of Accra's diversity, where locals and visitors alike engage in the timeless dance of commerce.

Jamestown, one of Accra's oldest districts, unfolds as a living canvas of history. The lighthouse, overlooking the Atlantic Ocean, offers panoramic views of the city and serves as a poignant reminder of Accra's maritime heritage. Graffiti-adorned walls narrate stories of the neighborhood's resilience, capturing the essence of a community that thrives amid urban transformation.

Cultural Enclaves

Accra is a city that treasures its cultural heritage, and this is evident in the myriad cultural enclaves that dot its landscape. The W.E.B. Du Bois Center, named after the renowned African American scholar and activist, is a sanctuary of intellectualism and Pan-Africanism. The mausoleum, where Du Bois and his wife rest, is a pilgrimage site for those seeking a deeper understanding of the intertwined histories of Africa and its diaspora.

The Kwame Nkrumah Mausoleum, dedicated to Ghana's first president, is a grand edifice nestled in lush surroundings. It not only commemorates Nkrumah's legacy but also serves as a space for reflection on Ghana's journey to independence. The surrounding park, adorned with statues and fountains, invites contemplation and appreciation for the leaders who paved the way for the nation's freedom.

Spiritual Sanctuaries

Accra's spiritual landscape is diverse, reflecting the religious pluralism that characterizes Ghana. The vibrant colors of the Osu Castle, also known as Christiansborg Castle, create a striking contrast against the azure sky. Originally built by the Danes, the castle has served various purposes throughout history, from a seat of government to a presidential residence. Today, it is a symbol of administrative authority and historical significance.

The Independence Square, with its monumental Black Star Gate, is a venue for national celebrations and events. Surrounded by the Independence Arch, the square is not only a space for civic gatherings but also a testament to the nation's commitment to freedom and self-determination.

Culinary Delights

Accra's culinary scene is a journey through flavors that reflect the nation's diverse cultural influences. From the aromatic spices of street-side waakye vendors to the savory goodness of fufu and light soups, Ghanaian cuisine is a celebration of indigenous ingredients and culinary creativity.

The vibrant Oxford Street in Osu is a gastronomic paradise, offering a medley of restaurants, cafes, and street food stalls. Here, you can indulge in local delicacies or savor international cuisines. Whether it's the fiery jollof rice, the succulent grilled tilapia, or the refreshing coconut water, Accra's culinary offerings are a delight for the discerning palate.

Art and Expression

Accra's artistic landscape is a canvas that reflects the city's creativity and expression. Nubuke Foundation, an art center nestled in the verdant landscape of East Legon, showcases contemporary Ghanaian art. From visual arts to performances, Nubuke is a haven for artists and art enthusiasts alike, fostering a dialogue between tradition and innovation.

Chale Wote Street Art Festival, held annually in Jamestown, transforms the neighborhood into an open-air gallery. The colorful murals, street performances, and interactive installations redefine Accra's streets, turning them into a vibrant tapestry of artistic expression.

Conclusion: Accra's Ever-Evolving Story

Accra is more than a city; it is a living narrative, a dynamic story that unfolds with each passing day. As you delve into the intricate weave of its streets, engage with its diverse communities, and savor its cultural offerings, you become part of Accra's ever-evolving tale.

This chapter, a mere introduction to Accra's multifaceted identity, invites you to delve deeper into the nuances of a city that encapsulates the spirit of a nation. Accra beckons, not just as a destination but as an immersive experience—an odyssey through history, culture, and the indomitable rhythm of urban life. As we embark on this exploration, remember that Accra's story is not static; it is a vibrant, pulsating narrative waiting to be discovered, one street, one market, and one monument at a time.

Chapter 2
The Cape Coast and Elmina - A Journey through History

Embarking on the coastal journey from Accra to Cape Coast and Elmina is not just a physical expedition; it is a passage through time. These historic enclaves, perched along the Gulf of Guinea, encapsulate the complexities of Ghana's past, bearing witness to the triumphs and tragedies that have shaped the nation's narrative.

Cape Coast: Echoes of the Past

As the road winds its way along the coastline, the distant silhouette of Cape Coast Castle emerges, an imposing structure that seems to defy the passage of time. This fortress, built by the Swedes in the 17th century and later expanded by the British, served as a linchpin in the trans-Atlantic slave trade. The castle, with its stark white walls overlooking the Atlantic Ocean, stands as a somber sentinel, a tangible link to a dark chapter in human history.

Venturing through the dungeons of Cape Coast Castle is a visceral experience. The cramped, dimly lit chambers bear witness to the inhumanity that transpired within these walls. The Door of No Return, a haunting portal through which enslaved Africans were forcibly transported onto waiting ships, is a poignant symbol of the human cost exacted by the slave trade. The museum within the castle provides a comprehensive narrative, detailing the intricacies of this tragic period and the resilience of those who endured.

Beyond its association with the slave trade, Cape Coast is a city that intertwines history with contemporary life. The Cape Coast Castle remains a focal point, a place of pilgrimage for those seeking to understand the depths of Ghana's past. The city itself, with its vibrant markets, colonial-era architecture, and the Cape Coast University, stands as a testament to the endurance of its people and their commitment to education and progress.

Elmina: A Tapestry of Trade and Conquest

A short distance from Cape Coast lies Elmina, a coastal town steeped in history that predates the arrival of European powers on the West African shores. Elmina Castle, constructed by the Portuguese in the late 15th century, is the oldest European building in sub-Saharan Africa. Originally established as a trade settlement, Elmina Castle became a key hub in the trans-Atlantic slave trade, changing hands between the Portuguese, Dutch, and British over the centuries.

Wandering through the corridors of Elmina Castle, the weight of history is palpable. The commodious courtyards, once bustling with commercial activities, now echo with the whispers of the past. The slave dungeons, akin to those in Cape Coast, bear witness to the unfathomable suffering endured by countless souls. The ominous cannon-lined walls, built for defense and control, provide a stark contrast to the serene beauty of the surrounding coastline.

Elmina's historical narrative extends beyond the castle walls. The town itself, with its lively fishing community and vibrant markets, reflects a resilience born out of centuries of trade, conquest, and cultural exchange. The St. George's Castle, an adjacent fortification built by the Portuguese, further enriches the historical tapestry, reminding visitors of the strategic importance of Elmina in the European quest for dominance in West Africa.

Reckoning with History: Reflections on the Present

The journey through Cape Coast and Elmina is not a mere exploration of architectural relics; it is a reckoning with history. It is an opportunity to confront the collective human capacity for both cruelty and resilience. These coastal enclaves, once epicenters of a brutal trade, now serve as memorials, urging contemplation on the legacy of colonialism and the impact of the trans-Atlantic slave trade on the African diaspora.

While the historical weight is undeniable, there is also a sense of resilience that permeates these sites. The very existence of these castles and forts, meticulously preserved and open to the public, is a testament to Ghana's commitment to historical remembrance. They stand as educational monuments, inviting dialogue on the complexities of the past and fostering a collective responsibility to ensure such atrocities are never repeated.

Moreover, these sites are not frozen in time; they exist within living communities. Cape Coast and Elmina, with their vibrant populations, bustling markets, and cultural richness, showcase a nation that has transcended the shadows of its history. The people of these coastal towns, heirs to a profound legacy, navigate the complexities of the present while preserving the threads of their cultural heritage.

Beyond the Fortifications: Exploring Coastal Communities

As visitors venture beyond the castle walls, they encounter coastal communities whose resilience mirrors the strength of the fortifications that dot the shoreline. Fishing villages, with their colorful boats lining the beaches, provide a glimpse into a way of life intricately connected to the sea. The rhythmic chants of fishermen hauling in their catch echo the centuries-old traditions that persist amid modernity.

Cape Coast and Elmina are not frozen in the past; they are thriving communities that have embraced the nuances of their history. The vibrant markets, where locals trade in everything from fresh produce to handmade crafts, exemplify the resilience and creativity that define these coastal towns. These markets are not just economic hubs; they are living reflections of the cultural diversity that has flourished along Ghana's coastline.

Conclusion: A Living History Lesson

Cape Coast and Elmina are not just historical sites; they are living history lessons. The journey through these coastal enclaves transcends the conventional tourist experience, inviting travelers to engage with the complexities of Ghana's past and reflect on the broader implications of colonialism and the slave trade.

As visitors stand on the ramparts of Cape Coast Castle, gaze out from Elmina's St. George's Castle, or walk along the shores where history unfolded, they are partaking in an odyssey that spans continents and centuries. The history of Cape Coast and Elmina is not isolated; it is interconnected with the broader narrative of the African diaspora and the global struggle for justice and equality.

In navigating these coastal chapters, one cannot help but be moved by the resilience of the human spirit and the profound capacity for transformation. Cape Coast and Elmina, with their storied pasts and vibrant presents, beckon travelers to not only witness history but to engage with it—to grapple with its complexities, to honor its victims, and to appreciate the resilience that defines the human experience. In doing so, visitors become not just spectators but participants in an ongoing narrative, contributing their reflections to the ever-evolving story of Cape Coast, Elmina, and the indomitable spirit of Ghana.

Chapter 3
Kumasi - The Cultural Hub

Nestled in the heart of the Ashanti Region, Kumasi emerges as a cultural epicenter, a city that breathes life into the traditions and legacies of the Ashanti Kingdom. As the historical capital of the Ashanti people, Kumasi is a living testament to the resilience, creativity, and cultural richness that define this vibrant community.

The Ashanti Kingdom: A Tapestry of Tradition

Kumasi is synonymous with the Ashanti Kingdom, a realm steeped in history and tradition. The Ashanti people, renowned for their artistry, military prowess, and intricate social structures, have left an indelible mark on the cultural landscape of Ghana. As you traverse the streets of Kumasi, the echoes of the kingdom's past resonate in every corner, from the majestic Manhyia Palace to the bustling markets of Kejetia.

The Manhyia Palace, seat of the Ashanti king, stands as a regal symbol of the kingdom's endurance. Originally built in 1925, the palace has undergone renovations, preserving its architectural grandeur while accommodating modern conveniences. Visitors are welcomed to explore the palace grounds, gaining insights into Ashanti history, governance, and the significance of the Golden Stool, a revered symbol of the kingdom's unity.

Kejetia Market: A Kaleidoscope of Commerce

Kumasi's Kejetia Market is not just a marketplace; it is a living entity, a pulsating hub of commerce and cultural exchange. Covering an expansive area in the city center, Kejetia is one of the largest markets in West Africa. The labyrinthine alleys and vibrant stalls create a sensory immersion into the rhythm of daily life.

Here, traders from across the Ashanti Region converge to showcase a kaleidoscope of goods, from handcrafted artifacts and traditional fabrics to spices, herbs, and fresh produce. Kejetia is not merely a place to buy and sell; it is a microcosm of Ashanti culture, where the art of negotiation, storytelling, and community interaction intertwines seamlessly.

Cultural Heritage at the Centre for National Culture

The Centre for National Culture, located in the heart of Kumasi, serves as a repository of Ghana's artistic heritage. This cultural hub is a celebration of traditional craftsmanship, music, dance, and visual arts. As visitors wander through its halls, they encounter a diverse array of artifacts, each narrating a story of cultural evolution and artistic expression.

The cultural center is a testament to the adaptability of traditional art forms. From Kente weaving, where vibrant patterns and colors convey stories and status, to Adinkra printing, a method of adorning fabric with symbolic motifs, the Centre for National Culture encapsulates the dynamic nature of Ashanti artistic traditions.

Adinkra Symbols: Language in Design

In Kumasi, the Adinkra symbols serve as an eloquent language embedded in design. These intricate symbols, with names like Sankofa (representing the importance of learning from the past) and Nkyinkyim (symbolizing initiative and versatility), adorn fabrics, pottery, and architecture. Each symbol encapsulates a proverbial message, adding layers of meaning to artistic expression.

The Ntonso Adinkra village, located near Kumasi, is renowned for its expertise in traditional Adinkra printing. Here, visitors have the opportunity to witness the meticulous process of carving symbols into stamps, applying them to fabric with natural dyes, and gaining a deeper understanding of the cultural significance woven into each design.

Ashanti Traditional Architecture: A Living Heritage

Kumasi's landscape is embellished with architectural gems that reflect the Ashanti people's reverence for tradition. The Kumasi Fort, built by the British in the 19th century and later utilized as a military base, is a testament to the city's historical importance. The fort, with its robust walls and strategic location, stands as a tangible reminder of the colonial era and the Ashanti resistance.

Additionally, the Kumasi Central Mosque, an architectural marvel, represents the diverse religious tapestry woven into the city's cultural fabric. Its intricate design, influenced by Islamic architectural styles, adds a layer of religious diversity to Kumasi's architectural narrative.

Ceremonial Splendor: Ashanti Festivals

Kumasi comes alive during Ashanti festivals, where the city's streets transform into vibrant stages for cultural expression. The Akwasidae Festival, celebrated every 42 days, is a grand occasion that draws locals and visitors alike. The Manhyia Palace becomes the focal point of the festivities, as the Ashanti king, adorned in regal attire, receives homage from dignitaries and the public.

Durbar grounds, adorned with traditional stools and symbols, host colorful parades, cultural displays, and rhythmic drumming. The atmosphere is infused with the scent of incense, the sounds of traditional music, and the sight of vibrant kente fabrics. The Akwasidae Festival is a sensory immersion into the living traditions of the Ashanti people, encapsulating the essence of Kumasi's cultural vibrancy.

Culinary Delights: Kumasi's Gastronomic Tapestry

Kumasi's culinary scene is a fusion of tradition and innovation, reflecting the city's dynamic cultural landscape. Traditional dishes such as fufu and light soup, banku and tilapia, and jollof rice are staples that celebrate local flavors. Street food vendors, with their aromatic offerings, provide a taste of Ashanti hospitality to those exploring Kumasi's streets.

Adum, the city's commercial center, is a culinary haven where local eateries offer an array of dishes. From the spicy aroma of waakye to the savory delights of kebabs, Adum is a microcosm of Kumasi's diverse gastronomic offerings. The communal spirit of dining, where locals and visitors share meals, adds a layer of conviviality to Kumasi's culinary tapestry.

Education and Innovation: Kumasi's Modern Identity

As the cultural hub of Ghana, Kumasi seamlessly integrates tradition with modernity. The Kwame Nkrumah University of Science and Technology (KNUST), located in Kumasi, exemplifies the city's commitment to education and innovation. The university, named after Ghana's first president, is a center for scientific research, technological advancement, and academic excellence.

KNUST's campus, adorned with sculptures and greenery, stands as a symbol of progress and intellectual pursuits. The university's influence extends beyond its academic endeavors; it contributes to Kumasi's vibrant cultural scene through artistic events, scientific exhibitions, and community engagement.

Conclusion: Kumasi's Living Legacy

Kumasi, the cultural hub of Ghana, is not merely a city; it is a living legacy. As visitors traverse its streets, engage with its artistic expressions, and participate in its festivals, they become part of a narrative that transcends time. Kumasi's cultural richness, manifested in its traditions, festivals, and artistic endeavors, invites exploration not as a passive observer but as an active participant in the ongoing story of the Ashanti Kingdom.

In Kumasi, history is not relegated to the past; it is an integral part of daily life. The city's inhabitants, proud custodians of their cultural heritage, weave the threads of tradition into the fabric of contemporary existence. Kumasi is a celebration of resilience, a testament to the enduring spirit of a people who have navigated the currents of time without losing sight of their roots.

As we conclude this exploration of Kumasi, may it inspire a deeper appreciation for the intricate tapestry of Ashanti culture and the city's role as a cultural nucleus in Ghana. Kumasi beckons travelers not just to witness but to engage—to dance to the rhythms of the Adowa, to savor the flavors of local cuisine, and to immerse themselves in a city where the past and present coalesce in a harmonious dance. In Kumasi, the cultural heartbeat of Ghana, every step is an invitation to be part of a living legacy, a journey that transcends the boundaries of time and leaves an indelible mark on the soul.

Chapter 4
Wildlife Wonders - Mole National Park

In the vast expanse of northern Ghana, Mole National Park unfolds as a wildlife haven, a sanctuary where the rhythms of nature dictate the daily narrative. This chapter invites you into the heart of Mole, where the undulating savannah, meandering rivers, and diverse ecosystems converge to create an unparalleled showcase of West African biodiversity.

The Landscape: A Tapestry of Savannas

Mole National Park sprawls over 4,577 square kilometers, making it the largest protected area in Ghana. The park's topography is characterized by a mosaic of savannas, woodlands, and riparian zones. As the landscape undulates, visitors are treated to panoramic views that extend to the horizon, offering a sense of vastness that belies the park's intricate ecosystems.

The Northern Region's arid climate shapes Mole's vegetation, fostering a blend of grasslands and acacia woodlands. The savannas, punctuated by baobab trees and elephant grass, provide an idyllic backdrop for wildlife sightings. Mole River, a lifeline for the park's inhabitants, meanders through the landscape, creating oases that sustain diverse flora and fauna.

Wildlife Spectacle: A Pantheon of Species

Mole National Park is a testament to the biodiversity that thrives in West Africa. The park is home to an impressive array of mammals, birds, reptiles, and insects, each playing a unique role in the intricate ecological web.

Elephants, the park's iconic inhabitants, roam freely across the savannas, creating an awe-inspiring sight. Mole is renowned for having one of the largest populations of elephants in West Africa, and witnessing these majestic creatures in their natural habitat is a highlight for visitors. The park's open savannas also provide an ideal setting for observing other herbivores, including kob antelopes, waterbucks, hartebeests, and oribi.

Predators, such as lions and leopards, add an element of drama to Mole's wildlife theater. While sightings of these elusive cats require patience and a bit of luck, the presence of these predators underscores the park's role as a balanced ecosystem.

Mole National Park is a birdwatcher's paradise, boasting over 300 bird species. Raptors, such as hooded vultures and African fish eagles, soar overhead, while ground-dwelling birds like ostriches and guinea fowls navigate the savannas. The park's diverse habitats, including wetlands and riverbanks, attract a variety of waterfowl, making it a haven for bird enthusiasts.

Reptiles, including Nile crocodiles and various snake species, inhabit the park's waterways and grasslands. The vibrant tapestry of insect life, from butterflies to beetles, contributes to the park's ecological diversity, underscoring the interconnectedness of its inhabitants.

The Elephant Experience: An Iconic Encounter

Encountering elephants in Mole National Park is an immersive experience that transcends the realm of ordinary wildlife observation. As the giants of the savanna gracefully traverse the landscape, their social interactions and familial bonds come to the forefront. The park's knowledgeable guides provide insights into elephant behavior, enabling visitors to appreciate the complex dynamics within these tight-knit family groups.

Mole's elephants are accustomed to human presence, allowing for safe and respectful wildlife viewing. Elephant safaris, guided by experienced rangers, provide an opportunity to witness these gentle giants up close. As the elephants graze, bathe, and interact, visitors become witnesses to the intricate social structures that define elephant communities.

The Elephant Conservation Program at Mole National Park plays a crucial role in monitoring and protecting the park's elephant population. Through research initiatives and community engagement, the program contributes to the conservation of this iconic species and the overall health of the park's ecosystem.

Exploring Mole: Safaris and Beyond

Mole National Park offers a variety of safari experiences designed to cater to different preferences and interests. Game drives, led by knowledgeable guides, provide an opportunity to explore the vastness of the savannas and encounter a myriad of wildlife species. Sunrise and sunset safaris, with the changing hues of the sky as a backdrop, offer a particularly enchanting atmosphere for wildlife observation.

Walking safaris provide a more intimate encounter with the park's flora and fauna. Accompanied by experienced guides, visitors can explore the intricacies of the savanna on foot, gaining a deeper understanding of the smaller creatures, plants, and ecosystems that contribute to Mole's ecological tapestry.

For those seeking a different perspective, the Mole River Safari offers a tranquil journey along the park's waterways. As the boat glides along the river, visitors can observe hippos, crocodiles, and a variety of birdlife in their natural habitat. The river safari provides a serene contrast to the more exhilarating experiences of the savanna safaris.

Beyond wildlife encounters, Mole National Park offers opportunities for cultural engagement. The Mognori Eco-Village, located near the park, provides a glimpse into the traditional lifestyle of the local community. Visitors can partake in cultural activities, including traditional dance, storytelling, and artisanal crafts, fostering a connection between tourism and community development.

Conservation Initiatives: Sustaining Biodiversity

Mole National Park is not merely a wildlife spectacle; it is a bastion of conservation efforts aimed at preserving West Africa's biodiversity. The Ghana Wildlife Society, in collaboration with government agencies and international organizations, plays a pivotal role in the park's conservation initiatives.

Anti-poaching patrols, community outreach programs, and scientific research contribute to the protection of Mole's wildlife. The park's rangers, equipped with knowledge and dedication, work tirelessly to combat illegal activities and ensure the safety of both wildlife and visitors.

Community engagement is a cornerstone of Mole's conservation strategy. By involving local communities in sustainable tourism practices, the park aims to create a harmonious relationship between conservation and livelihoods. Education and awareness programs empower communities to become stewards of their natural heritage, fostering a sense of responsibility for the well-being of the park and its inhabitants.

Accommodations: Immerse in Nature

Mole National Park offers a range of accommodations that blend seamlessly with the natural surroundings, providing visitors with an immersive experience. Lodges situated within the park, such as the Mole Motel and Zaina Lodge, offer comfortable amenities and panoramic views of the savannas. Staying within the park allows visitors to be in close proximity to wildlife, with the sounds of the bush serving as a lullaby under the starlit sky.

The eco-friendly design of accommodations at Mole National Park reflects a commitment to sustainable tourism. Solar power, water conservation measures, and waste management initiatives contribute to minimizing the environmental footprint of visitors, ensuring that the park remains a haven for wildlife for generations to come.

Conclusion: Mole's Enduring Legacy

Mole National Park is not merely a destination for wildlife enthusiasts; it is a testament to the delicate balance between humanity and nature. As visitors traverse its landscapes, witness the majesty of elephants, and engage with the park's conservation initiatives, they become participants in a narrative that extends beyond the boundaries of Ghana.

Mole is a living testament to the resilience of West African biodiversity and the potential for harmonious coexistence between humans and wildlife. Through careful conservation efforts, community engagement, and sustainable tourism practices, Mole National Park stands as a beacon of hope—a sanctuary where the wonders of the natural world can be experienced and appreciated.

This chapter is an invitation to explore Mole's wildlife wonders, to witness the interconnectedness of ecosystems, and to embrace the responsibility we bear as stewards of this remarkable corner of the Earth. In Mole National Park, nature unfolds in its most authentic form, and every visit is a step toward ensuring that the legacy of this natural wonder endures for generations to come.

Chapter 5
Kakum National Park - Canopy Walk and Beyond

In the heart of the Central Region of Ghana, Kakum National Park stands as a testament to the country's commitment to preserving its natural heritage. While renowned for its iconic canopy walkway, Kakum is much more than a thrilling treetop experience. This chapter invites you to delve into the depths of Kakum, exploring its diverse ecosystems, rich biodiversity, and the unique conservation efforts that make it a jewel in Ghana's environmental crown.

The Canopy Walkway: A Sky-High Adventure

The crown jewel of Kakum National Park is undoubtedly its canopy walkway—a marvel of engineering that offers visitors a unique perspective on the rainforest ecosystem. Suspended between giant trees, the walkway elevates visitors to the treetops, providing an immersive experience amidst the verdant canopy.

The walkway consists of seven bridges, each varying in length and height, creating a network that spans over 300 meters. As visitors traverse these swaying bridges, they are enveloped in the sights and sounds of the rainforest, from the rustling leaves of towering trees to the distant calls of exotic birds. The canopy walkway is a thrilling adventure that not only showcases the breathtaking biodiversity of Kakum but also underscores the importance of canopy ecosystems in rainforest conservation.

Biodiversity in Kakum: A Symphony of Life

Beyond the exhilarating canopy walk, Kakum National Park boasts a rich tapestry of biodiversity within its 357 square kilometers. The park encompasses a variety of ecosystems, including primary rainforest, secondary forest, and savanna, creating a haven for a diverse array of flora and fauna.

Kakum is home to over 400 species of birds, making it a paradise for birdwatchers. The call of the hornbill, the melodious song of the turaco, and the vibrant plumage of the sunbird create a symphony of avian life that resonates through the rainforest. Ornithologists and casual bird enthusiasts alike can marvel at the diversity of species that inhabit Kakum's lush canopies.

Mammals, both large and small, add to the park's charismatic fauna. Antelopes, forest elephants, and duikers roam the understory, while primates such as colobus monkeys and the endangered Diana monkey swing from branch to branch. The park's elusive residents, including leopards and forest buffalo, contribute to the aura of wilderness that defines Kakum.

Kakum National Park is also a sanctuary for a myriad of insect species, amphibians, and reptiles. From colorful butterflies to cryptic chameleons, the park's rich insect and herpetofauna diversity adds layers of intrigue to the rainforest experience. For those with a penchant for botanical wonders, Kakum's forest floor is adorned with a plethora of plant species, including medicinal plants and towering hardwoods that have stood for centuries.

Conservation and Research in Kakum: Sustaining the Rainforest Legacy

Kakum National Park is not only a refuge for biodiversity but also a hub for scientific research and conservation initiatives. The park collaborates with local and international organizations to monitor wildlife populations, study forest dynamics, and implement sustainable resource management practices.

Research conducted in Kakum contributes valuable insights into the ecology of tropical rainforests and informs conservation strategies. Through partnerships with academic institutions and environmental agencies, the park plays a vital role in advancing our understanding of West African ecosystems and the challenges they face.

One notable initiative is Kakum's involvement in the African Tropical Rainforest Conservation and Sustainable Use (ARTS) program. This collaborative effort aims to enhance the conservation and sustainable use of tropical rainforests in Africa, addressing threats such as deforestation, climate change, and illegal logging. By participating in ARTS, Kakum National Park becomes part of a broader network dedicated to safeguarding the ecological integrity of Africa's rainforests.

Community Engagement and Sustainable Tourism

Kakum National Park recognizes the importance of engaging local communities in conservation efforts. The park's management collaborates with nearby villages to promote sustainable tourism practices, emphasizing the value of the rainforest as a community asset. Through community outreach programs, educational initiatives, and revenue-sharing arrangements, Kakum strives to ensure that local residents are active participants in the park's conservation mission.

Sustainable tourism practices are woven into the fabric of Kakum's operations. The park seeks to minimize its environmental impact by implementing measures such as waste reduction, energy conservation, and eco-friendly infrastructure. By adopting responsible tourism practices, Kakum National Park endeavors to strike a balance between providing memorable experiences for visitors and preserving the ecological integrity of the rainforest.

Interpretive Centers and Educational Programs

Kakum National Park enhances the visitor experience through interpretive centers that offer insights into the rainforest's ecological importance and the challenges it faces. Educational programs, guided tours, and interactive exhibits provide visitors with a deeper understanding of the interconnected relationships that sustain the park's biodiversity.

The Kakum Environmental Education Center serves as a focal point for educational activities, welcoming students, researchers, and the general public. Through workshops, lectures, and hands-on experiences, the center fosters environmental literacy and a sense of stewardship for

Ghana's natural heritage. By inspiring the next generation of conservationists, Kakum contributes to the long-term sustainability of the rainforest ecosystem.

Beyond the Canopy Walk: Exploring Kakum's Trails

While the canopy walkway is a highlight of Kakum National Park, the exploration doesn't end there. The park offers a network of hiking trails that cater to varying levels of fitness and time constraints. These trails lead visitors through diverse habitats, allowing for a more immersive experience in the rainforest.

The Assin Attandanso Trail, named after a nearby village, provides a gentle introduction to Kakum's biodiversity. This relatively short trail winds through the forest, offering opportunities to spot birds, butterflies, and small mammals. Interpretive signage along the trail enhances the educational aspect of the journey.

For those seeking a more extended adventure, the Otumedem Trail takes hikers deeper into the heart of the rainforest. This trail offers a chance to encounter larger wildlife species, experience the soundscape of the forest, and witness the complex interactions between flora and fauna. The Otumedem Trail is a journey into the heart of Kakum's ecological intricacies.

Camping in the Wilderness: Overnight Experiences

For an immersive rainforest experience, Kakum National Park provides camping facilities that allow visitors to spend a night in the heart of the wilderness. Camping in Kakum is a unique opportunity to fully appreciate the nocturnal symphony of the rainforest, as well as the chance to observe creatures that come to life under the cover of darkness.

Guided night walks offer a different perspective, revealing the hidden wonders of Kakum that are often elusive during daylight hours. The park's knowledgeable guides lead visitors through the rainforest, highlighting the sights and sounds of the nocturnal world. From the calls of tree frogs to the reflective eyes of nocturnal mammals, the night walk is a sensory adventure that adds a layer of mystery to the Kakum experience.

Conclusion: Kakum's Green Legacy

Kakum National Park stands as a verdant testament to Ghana's dedication to preserving its natural heritage. Beyond the adrenaline-inducing canopy walk, Kakum offers a journey into the heart of one of the world's most vital ecosystems—the tropical rainforest. As visitors traverse its trails, gaze upon its towering trees, and witness the intricate dance of life within its bounds, they become part of a legacy that extends beyond individual experiences.

Kakum's commitment to conservation, research, and community engagement sets it apart as a model for sustainable ecotourism. The park's lush landscapes and diverse inhabitants beckon visitors to not only marvel at nature's wonders but also to reflect on the importance of safeguarding these irreplaceable ecosystems.

In Kakum National Park, the treetop vistas of the canopy walk are a metaphor for the park's overarching mission—to elevate our understanding of the rainforest, to bridge the gap between human and nature, and to inspire a collective commitment to the preservation of Earth's green lungs. As we conclude our exploration of Kakum, may it serve as a lasting reminder of the beauty, complexity, and fragility of the rainforest—a legacy to be cherished, protected, and passed on to future generations.

Chapter 6
The Volta Region - Serenity by the Lake

Nestled in the eastern part of Ghana, the Volta Region unfolds as a landscape of captivating diversity, where the serene waters of Lake Volta meet lush hills and fertile valleys. This chapter invites you to embark on a journey through the Volta Region, a destination that harmonizes natural beauty, cultural richness, and a tranquil ambiance that sets it apart as a gem in West Africa.

Lake Volta: A Watery Tapestry

Lake Volta, one of the largest artificial lakes in the world, is a defining feature of the Volta Region. Created by the construction of the Akosombo Dam on the Volta River, the lake spans over 8,500 square kilometers, weaving its way through the undulating landscapes of the region. The expansive waters of Lake Volta are not only a source of hydroelectric power but also a canvas on which the daily life and rhythms of the communities along its shores unfold.

As you approach the lake, the air becomes infused with a sense of tranquility. Fishing boats glide across the water's surface, their colorful sails creating a picturesque tableau against the backdrop of the distant hills. The lake, with its myriad inlets and coves, provides a serene setting for reflection, relaxation, and the appreciation of the natural beauty that characterizes the Volta Region.

Akosombo Dam: Engineering Marvel Amidst Nature's Bounty

At the heart of Lake Volta stands the Akosombo Dam, a testament to human ingenuity and the symbiotic relationship between nature and infrastructure. The dam, completed in 1965, not only harnesses the power of the Volta River for electricity generation but also shapes the landscapes that cradle the lake.

The dam's viewing platform offers a panoramic vista that encapsulates the scale of Lake Volta and the surrounding hills. Visitors can witness the controlled release of water through the dam's spillways, a spectacle that underscores the delicate balance between harnessing natural resources and preserving the ecological integrity of the region.

Wli Waterfalls: Cascading Majesty in the Heart of Nature

Venturing into the lush interior of the Volta Region, the Wli Waterfalls beckon with their cascading majesty. Situated near the town of Hohoe, the waterfalls are a natural wonder that epitomizes the region's scenic diversity. The journey to Wli takes visitors through verdant landscapes, passing by traditional villages and fertile farmlands.

Upon reaching the falls, the sound of rushing water becomes a melodic backdrop to the natural amphitheater that unfolds. The Wli Waterfalls, comprising an upper and lower fall, plunge from towering heights, creating a refreshing mist that revitalizes the surrounding vegetation. The basin at the foot of the falls invites visitors to bask in the cool embrace of nature, fostering a sense of serenity that permeates the entire region.

Mount Afadja: Summiting West Africa's Tallest Peak

Rising majestically in the Akwapim-Togo mountain range, Mount Afadja stands as the highest peak in West Africa. The ascent to its summit, though challenging, rewards intrepid hikers with panoramic views that stretch across the Volta Region and beyond. The trail to the summit winds through lush forests, revealing a tapestry of biodiversity that thrives in the mountainous terrain.

Reaching the summit of Mount Afadja is a metaphorical ascent into the heart of the Volta Region's natural grandeur. The cool mountain air, the panoramic views of Lake Volta, and the sense of accomplishment at the peak create a profound connection between the visitor and the landscapes that define this corner of Ghana.

Tafi Atome Monkey Sanctuary: Harmony with Nature

The Volta Region is not only a haven for scenic landscapes but also a place where human communities coexist harmoniously with nature. The Tafi Atome Monkey Sanctuary exemplifies this delicate balance, where sacred monkeys roam freely in a community that regards them with reverence and protection.

The sanctuary is home to the Mona monkeys, a species known for their distinctive black fur and long tails. The villagers of Tafi Atome consider these monkeys sacred, believing them to be spiritual beings that bring blessings to the community. Visitors to the sanctuary can observe the monkeys in their natural habitat, guided by locals who share insights into the cultural significance of this unique coexistence.

Adaklu Mountain: Hiking to Tranquility

For those seeking a tranquil retreat amidst nature, the Adaklu Mountain offers a serene escape. The mountain, with its gentle slopes and scenic vistas, is a haven for hikers and nature enthusiasts. The trails leading to the summit meander through forests, passing by waterfalls and meadows that invite contemplation and relaxation.

The panoramic views from Adaklu Mountain stretch across the undulating landscapes of the Volta Region. The sense of serenity that pervades the mountain's slopes creates a therapeutic escape, inviting visitors to immerse themselves in the tranquility of nature.

Cultural Riches: Beyond Nature's Embrace

The Volta Region's allure extends beyond its natural wonders; it is also a repository of cultural richness and traditions. The region is home to various ethnic groups, each with its unique customs, languages, and artistic expressions. The Ewe people, predominant in the region, contribute to the cultural tapestry through their vibrant festivals, music, and dance.

Festivals such as the Hogbetsotso Festival, celebrated by the Anlo Ewe people, showcase the region's cultural dynamism. These festivals, marked by colorful parades, traditional dances, and communal celebrations, provide visitors with a window into the traditions that define life in the Volta Region.

Ghana's Eco-Village: The Experience at Wli

Wli, a community near the Wli Waterfalls, stands out as an exemplar of sustainable living and ecotourism. The village, surrounded by lush landscapes, offers visitors an opportunity to experience traditional Ewe culture while embracing eco-friendly practices.

Accommodations in Wli range from community-based guesthouses to eco-friendly lodges that prioritize sustainability. Visitors can engage in cultural exchanges with the locals, partake in traditional dances, and savor local cuisine prepared with ingredients sourced from the surrounding landscapes. The experience at Wli goes beyond typical tourism; it is an immersion into a community that values the preservation of its natural and cultural heritage.

Conclusion: The Volta Region's Timeless Appeal

As we conclude our exploration of the Volta Region, its timeless appeal becomes evident. This corner of Ghana is not merely a destination; it is a testament to the delicate dance between nature and human communities, a symphony of landscapes, and a canvas upon which cultural traditions are painted.

The serenity of Lake Volta, the majestic waterfalls, the heights of Mount Afadja, and the cultural richness of the region create an immersive experience that transcends the ordinary. The Volta Region invites visitors to not only witness its natural and cultural wonders but to become part of a narrative that unfolds amidst the hills, valleys, and waters that define this enchanting corner of West Africa.

In the Volta Region, serenity is not just a state of being; it is a way of life—a connection between humanity and the natural world that has endured through generations. As travelers venture through its landscapes, may they find not only the beauty that captivates the senses but also the timeless spirit that makes the Volta Region a destination where serenity is not just a fleeting moment but a lasting embrace.

Chapter 7
Beyond Borders - Togo and Côte d'Ivoire

Ghana, with its rich cultural heritage and diverse landscapes, shares its borders with two unique nations—Togo to the east and Côte d'Ivoire to the west. This chapter delves into the transcendent appeal of exploring the neighboring countries, each offering a distinctive tapestry of experiences that complement the cultural and natural wonders of Ghana.

Togo: A Tapestry of Tradition and Nature

Just beyond Ghana's eastern border lies Togo, a nation that captivates with its blend of traditional cultures, vibrant markets, and breathtaking landscapes. From the bustling capital city of Lomé to the rural villages nestled in the hills, Togo invites travelers to explore a country where traditions thrive amidst a backdrop of natural beauty.

Lomé, a coastal city with a colonial legacy, introduces visitors to Togo's urban rhythm. The Grand Marché, a bustling market in the heart of the city, is a sensory immersion into West African commerce. Stalls brim with textiles, crafts, and spices, creating a kaleidoscope of colors and aromas. The vibrant atmosphere reflects Lomé's status as a cultural crossroads, where influences from various ethnic groups converge.

Heading northward, the landscape transforms into a mosaic of hills, valleys, and traditional villages. The Tamberma Valley, home to the Tamberma people, is renowned for its distinctive Tata Somba houses. These fortress-like structures, made of mud and wood, stand as architectural marvels that blend seamlessly with the rugged terrain. Exploring the Tamberma Valley is a journey through time, offering insights into the age-old traditions of the Tamberma people.

Further north, the Koutammakou landscape, a UNESCO World Heritage Site, beckons with its iconic mud tower-houses and terraced fields. The Batammariba people, who inhabit this region, maintain a harmonious relationship with the land, preserving their cultural practices in the face of modernization. The Koutammakou landscape is not just a testament to architectural ingenuity but also a living heritage where traditions endure.

Togo's natural wonders extend beyond its cultural landscapes. The Fazao-Malfakassa National Park, with its dense forests and diverse wildlife, offers a refuge for nature enthusiasts. Exploring the park's trails reveals a wealth of flora and fauna, from towering trees to elusive primates. The park is a sanctuary where the symphony of birdsong and the rustling of leaves create a serene escape into Togo's wilderness.

Côte d'Ivoire: The Jewel of the West

To the west of Ghana, Côte d'Ivoire emerges as a jewel that blends modernity with a rich cultural legacy. Abidjan, the economic capital, stands as a testament to the country's urban dynamism. Skyscrapers, bustling markets, and a vibrant arts scene characterize Abidjan, creating a cityscape that mirrors Côte d'Ivoire's embrace of progress.

The Plateau district, Abidjan's central business hub, is a showcase of modern architecture and commerce. The St. Paul's Cathedral, with its striking design, and the Banco National Park, a pocket of greenery within the city, add layers of cultural and natural appeal to the urban landscape. Abidjan's cultural vibrancy is exemplified by the Treichville district, where street art, music, and dance converge to create a lively atmosphere.

The Grand Bassam, a UNESCO World Heritage Site, beckons travelers to the historic heart of Côte d'Ivoire. This coastal town, with its colonial-era architecture and serene beaches, invites reflection on the country's complex history. The Grand Bassam stands as a living museum, where the echoes of the past resonate through cobblestone streets and centuries-old buildings.

Heading north from Abidjan, the cityscape gives way to the lush landscapes of Côte d'Ivoire's interior. Yamoussoukro, the political capital, surprises visitors with its grandeur. The Basilica of Our Lady of Peace, one of the largest churches in the world, dominates the city's skyline. Set amidst manicured gardens and reflective pools, the basilica is a symbol of Côte d'Ivoire's cultural aspirations.

Côte d'Ivoire's natural beauty extends to Tai National Park, a haven for biodiversity in the southwest. The park's dense forests, waterfalls, and diverse ecosystems provide a refuge for rare species such as pygmy hippos, chimpanzees, and the endangered olive colobus monkeys. Exploring Tai National Park is a journey into the heart of West Africa's wilderness, where the rhythm of nature unfolds undisturbed.

Crossing Borders: The Interconnected Tapestry

Embarking on a journey that transcends borders—venturing from Ghana into Togo and Côte d'Ivoire—reveals the interconnected tapestry of West African cultures and landscapes. The borders that demarcate nations become permeable membranes through which the essence of the region flows seamlessly.

The shared history, cultural exchanges, and natural wonders that define this corner of West Africa are evident as travelers traverse from one nation to another. The marketplaces of Lomé echo the vibrancy of Grand Marché in Accra, while the mud tower-houses of the Tamberma Valley resonate with the architectural heritage of the Volta Region. The cosmopolitan allure of Abidjan finds echoes in Accra's urban energy, creating a continuum of cultural expression that extends beyond geopolitical boundaries.

Exploring Togo and Côte d'Ivoire alongside Ghana enriches the narrative of West Africa's diversity. The journey becomes a symphony of languages, cuisines, artistic expressions, and natural wonders that harmonize to create an immersive experience. Each nation, with its unique character, contributes to the collective identity of the region, a testament to the shared heritage that transcends political divisions.

Traveling Responsibly: A Call to Conservation

As travelers navigate the landscapes of West Africa, including Ghana, Togo, and Côte d'Ivoire, a responsibility emerges—a duty to preserve and protect the cultural and natural heritage that makes this region exceptional. Sustainable tourism practices become a compass, guiding the way toward experiences that leave a positive impact on communities and ecosystems.

Engaging with local communities respectfully, supporting sustainable initiatives, and treading lightly on the natural landscapes are integral aspects of responsible travel. Conservation of cultural heritage, whether manifested in traditional practices or historic sites, becomes a shared endeavor that bridges the past with the present and safeguards the legacy for future generations.

In traversing borders and experiencing the interconnected tapestry of West Africa, travelers become stewards of a living heritage. The call to conservation is not merely a responsibility; it is an invitation to be part of a narrative that transcends borders—a journey that celebrates the richness of cultures, the diversity of landscapes, and the timeless allure of this corner of the African continent.

Chapter 8
Ghanaian Cuisine - A Gastronomic Odyssey

Embarking on a journey through the culinary landscape of Ghana is akin to setting sail on a gastronomic odyssey. The nation's cuisine is a tapestry woven with diverse flavors, vibrant colors, and a rich cultural heritage. From the bustling markets of Accra to the coastal villages of Cape Coast, Ghanaian cuisine unfolds as a sensory experience that mirrors the country's history, geography, and the warm hospitality of its people.

Foundations of Ghanaian Cuisine: A Culinary Mosaic

At the heart of Ghanaian cuisine lies a deep-rooted connection to the land. The culinary traditions draw inspiration from the diverse ecosystems that define the country—lush forests, fertile plains, and the bountiful Atlantic coastline. Ghanaian dishes are a reflection of the agricultural abundance, with staples such as cassava, yams, plantains, and cocoyams forming the foundation of many meals.

The culinary mosaic extends to protein sources, where fish, poultry, and various meats play prominent roles. Along the coast, where the Atlantic Ocean meets the shores of Ghana, fresh seafood takes center stage. Inland, the bounty of the savannah contributes to the richness of the cuisine with a variety of meats, including beef, goat, and lamb.

Ghanaian cuisine is also characterized by the imaginative use of spices and herbs. From the fiery kick of chili peppers to the aromatic blend of ginger, garlic, and an array of local spices, each dish is an intricate dance of flavors. The use of palm oil, groundnuts, and coconut milk adds depth and richness to many Ghanaian dishes, creating a harmonious blend of tastes that titillate the palate.

Staples of Ghanaian Cuisine: The Heart of the Plate

A journey into Ghanaian cuisine reveals a delectable array of staples that form the heart of many meals. One such staple is jollof rice, a dish that transcends its role as mere sustenance to become a cultural symbol. Prepared with rice, tomatoes, onions, and an assortment of spices, jollof rice is a celebration of flavors that varies from region to region, each household adding its unique touch to this iconic dish.

Banku and fufu, both made from fermented starchy ingredients like cassava, yams, or plantains, are versatile staples that accompany a myriad of dishes. These dough-like substances are often served with soups, stews, or sauces, creating a textural and flavorful contrast that defines many traditional Ghanaian meals.

The waakye, a dish characterized by rice cooked with millet leaves, exemplifies the resourcefulness of Ghanaian cuisine. The addition of sorghum leaves gives the rice a distinct reddish-brown color, and the dish is often accompanied by a variety of sides, including boiled eggs, spaghetti, and fish.

Gari, a granular flour made from cassava, is another ubiquitous staple in Ghanaian cuisine. It serves as a base for various dishes, including gari foto, a popular street food made with gari, vegetables, and protein sources such as fish or meat.

Seafood Delights: Exploring Coastal Cuisines

Ghana's extensive coastline blesses its cuisine with an abundance of fresh seafood, enriching the culinary tapestry with flavors from the Atlantic. The bustling fish markets along the coast offer a vibrant display of the day's catch, setting the stage for dishes that capture the essence of coastal living.

Grilled tilapia, seasoned with a medley of spices and herbs, is a quintessential Ghanaian seafood delicacy. Served with a side of pepper sauce and plantains, this dish is a testament to the country's ability to elevate simple ingredients into a gastronomic masterpiece. Lightly smoked fish, such as the popular smoked mackerel, infuses a distinctive flavor into soups, stews, and rice dishes.

Banku and tilapia, a classic combination, epitomize the synergy between staple foods and seafood. The fermented banku, paired with the grilled tilapia and a spicy pepper sauce, creates a symphony of textures and tastes that captures the essence of coastal living.

Light soups, prepared with an assortment of seafood, vegetables, and aromatic spices, offer a refreshing and nutritious culinary experience. The incorporation of okra, garden eggs, and spinach adds a wholesome dimension to these soups, creating a balance between flavors and nutritional value.

Street Food: Culinary Adventures in Every Bite

Ghana's street food culture is a vibrant testament to the nation's culinary creativity and the spirit of communal dining. From bustling urban markets to quaint roadside stalls, the aroma of sizzling pans and the allure of flavorful bites beckon locals and visitors alike to partake in the joys of street food.

Kelewele, a beloved street food snack, consists of spicy, fried plantains seasoned with a blend of ginger, chili, and other spices. The juxtaposition of sweetness from the ripe plantains and the heat from the spices creates a harmonious explosion of flavors in every bite.

Waakye, often found at street food vendors, showcases the versatility of this traditional dish. Served with a variety of accompaniments, including boiled eggs, spaghetti, and fish or meat, waakye is a complete meal that captures the essence of Ghanaian street food.

Suya, inspired by West African flavors, is a grilled meat delicacy that has found a home on the streets of Ghana. Thinly sliced meat, often beef or chicken, is marinated in a spicy blend of ground peanuts, chili, and other spices before being skewered and grilled to perfection.

Traditional Dishes: Celebrating Culinary Heritage

Ghanaian cuisine is a celebration of culinary heritage, and traditional dishes play a pivotal role in preserving and passing on cultural legacies. One such dish is fufu and light soup, a combination that transcends mere sustenance to become a cultural expression of communal dining.

Fufu, made from cassava, yams, or plantains, is pounded to a smooth consistency and served alongside light soups made with fish, meat, or vegetables. The communal act of pounding fufu, often done in groups, is a social event that brings people together to share in the preparation and enjoyment of a wholesome meal.

Another iconic dish is groundnut soup with rice balls, a culinary delight that embodies the rich flavors of Ghanaian cuisine. The groundnut soup, made with peanuts, tomatoes, and an array of spices, creates a velvety and aromatic base for the rice balls. The combination of textures and tastes in this dish reflects the country's commitment to culinary diversity.

Sweet Endings: Desserts and Sweets

No culinary odyssey is complete without indulging in the sweet offerings of a nation's desserts. Ghanaian sweets and desserts are a delightful conclusion to a gastronomic journey, showcasing the country's penchant for incorporating tropical fruits and flavors into its confections.

Keenam, a traditional Ghanaian dessert, is a sweet and sticky delicacy made from millet flour, sugar, and water. This confection is often enjoyed during festive occasions and celebrations, adding a touch of sweetness to communal gatherings.

Plantain chips, both sweet and savory, are a popular snack that combines the natural sweetness of ripe plantains with a hint of salt or sugar. Whether enjoyed on their own or as a side to savory dishes, plantain chips offer a satisfying crunch and a burst of flavor.

Beverages: Navigating Ghana's Liquid Landscape

Ghana's liquid landscape is as diverse as its culinary offerings, with a range of beverages that cater to different preferences and occasions. From traditional drinks to modern concoctions, Ghanaian beverages are a refreshing exploration of local ingredients and cultural influences.

Sobolo, a hibiscus-based drink, is a ubiquitous presence at gatherings and events. The deep red beverage is made by steeping dried hibiscus petals in water, often flavored with ginger and other spices. Sobolo is not only a refreshing thirst-quencher but also a cultural symbol of hospitality and conviviality.

Palm wine, tapped from the sap of palm trees, holds a special place in Ghanaian culture. The mildly alcoholic beverage is enjoyed in social settings and celebrations, offering a taste of the country's natural bounty.

In recent years, the burgeoning popularity of traditional drinks has been complemented by a rise in modern and innovative beverages. Fruit juices, smoothies, and locally inspired cocktails showcase Ghana's ability to blend tradition with contemporary tastes, offering a diverse array of options for both locals and visitors.

Culinary Heritage as a Cultural Ambassador

Ghanaian cuisine serves as a cultural ambassador, transcending borders and inviting people from diverse backgrounds to partake in the nation's culinary heritage. As travelers embark on a gastronomic odyssey through the markets, street food stalls, and traditional kitchens of Ghana, they become participants in a narrative that extends beyond the plate.

The act of sharing meals becomes a bridge between cultures, a means of understanding the history, values, and traditions that define Ghanaian identity. Whether savoring the complex flavors of jollof rice, partaking in the communal ritual of fufu preparation, or enjoying the sweet endings of Ghanaian desserts, each bite is a journey into the heart of the nation.

Ghanaian cuisine embodies the spirit of hospitality, where meals are not merely sustenance but a manifestation of community, celebration, and the warmth of human connection. As we conclude our gastronomic odyssey through Ghana, may the memories of flavors linger, and the appreciation for the country's culinary heritage endure as a testament to the richness of this vibrant and inviting nation.

Chapter 9
Festivals and Celebrations

Ghana, a nation steeped in rich cultural traditions, pulsates with a vibrant tapestry of festivals and celebrations throughout the year. These events are more than mere spectacles; they are living expressions of the country's diverse ethnicities, ancient rituals, and the dynamic rhythm of its people. As we delve into the kaleidoscope of Ghanaian festivals, we uncover a narrative that transcends time, weaving together the threads of history, spirituality, and communal joy.

The Rhythms of Adowa: Celebrating Asante Heritage

The Adowa Festival, celebrated by the Asante people, stands as a testament to the resilience and cultural richness of one of Ghana's prominent ethnic groups. This festival, dedicated to honoring the bravery of the Asante warriors, is a dynamic showcase of traditional music, dance, and spiritual rituals.

The beating of drums, adorned with intricate patterns and imbued with historical significance, echoes through the air. The dancers, draped in vibrant kente cloth and adorned with symbolic accessories, move in rhythmic unison, their steps telling stories of triumph and heritage. The Adowa Festival is not only a celebration of Asante identity but also an homage to the ancestors who shaped the course of the nation's history.

Homowo: Harvesting Traditions in Ga-Dangme Culture

In the Ga-Dangme culture, the Homowo Festival emerges as a time-honored celebration of agricultural abundance and the triumph over adversity. The word "Homowo" translates to "hooting at hunger," and the festival's origins can be traced to a period of famine that the Ga-Dangme people overcame through unity and resilience.

The festival commences with the planting of millet, symbolizing the beginning of the planting season. The climactic event involves the harvesting of the first crops, accompanied by vibrant processions, drumming, and dancing. The joyful clamor of the Homowo Festival is a communal expression of gratitude for the bountiful harvest and a reflection on the shared strength that sustains the Ga-Dangme people.

Panafest: A Pan-African Celebration in Cape Coast

Panafest, short for the Pan-African Historical Theatre Festival, is a biennial event held in Cape Coast that transcends national borders to embrace the broader African diaspora. This festival, established in 1992, serves as a platform for cultural exchange, historical reflection, and a reconnection to African roots.

Panafest brings together people from various African nations and the diaspora to celebrate the resilience, creativity, and shared heritage of the African continent. The event features a diverse array of activities, including theater performances, music and dance showcases, academic symposiums, and a durbar—a colorful gathering of traditional leaders, dignitaries, and the public. Panafest serves as a poignant reminder of the interconnected histories and shared destinies that bind people of African descent across the globe.

Damba Festival: A Northern Celebration of Spiritual Significance

In the northern regions of Ghana, the Damba Festival holds sway as a vibrant expression of Islamic traditions and cultural heritage. Celebrated by the Dagombas, Mamprusis, and Nanumbas, the festival revolves around the remembrance of the birth and life of the Islamic prophet, Muhammad.

The festivities encompass a series of events, including traditional drumming, dancing, and horse riding. The highlight of the Damba Festival is the procession of the "Yaa Naa," the paramount chief, and his retinue. This colorful and ceremonious procession through the streets is a visual spectacle that captures the spiritual significance of the festival and reflects the unity and cultural identity of the northern communities.

Akwantukese: Harvesting with the Akuapem People

In the Akuapem culture, the Akwantukese Festival is a celebration of the harvest season, marked by traditional rituals and communal festivities. The festival is a time for reflection on the agricultural cycle, gratitude for the harvest, and the strengthening of social bonds within the community.

The Akwantukese Festival features a durbar of chiefs and elders, cultural performances, and a showcase of traditional crafts and cuisine. The rhythmic sounds of traditional drums set the pace for dancing and merriment, creating an atmosphere of jubilation as the community comes together to celebrate the abundance provided by the land.

Kundum Festival: A Western Tradition of Renewal

The Kundum Festival, celebrated by the Ahanta and Nzema people in the Western Region, is a vibrant expression of cultural renewal, spiritual cleansing, and community bonding. The festival, which usually spans several weeks, involves a series of events that culminate in a grand celebration marked by traditional music, dance, and spiritual rituals.

A distinctive feature of the Kundum Festival is the "firing of muskets" ceremony, where muskets are fired to purify the community and ward off evil spirits. The festival also includes a procession of chiefs and elders, the display of traditional regalia, and the performance of ancestral rites. Kundum serves as a testament to the resilience of the Western Region's cultural heritage and its commitment to preserving age-old traditions.

Aboakyer: The Deer Hunting Festival of the Efutu People

The Aboakyer Festival, celebrated by the Efutu people in Winneba, is a unique and captivating event that combines elements of traditional spirituality, hunting prowess, and community participation. The festival, dating back over three centuries, revolves around the symbolic hunting of a deer—a ritual that signifies the community's ability to overcome challenges and ensure prosperity.

The Aboakyer Festival begins with the catching of the deer by the "Asafo" warriors, a group of skilled hunters. The captured deer is then presented to the paramount chief as a symbol of victory. The festival includes colorful processions, drumming, dancing, and a communal feast. Aboakyer not only celebrates the resilience of the Efutu people but also fosters a sense of unity and shared identity.

Fetu Afahye: The Grand Durbar of the Cape Coast People

Fetu Afahye, celebrated in Cape Coast, is an annual festival that pays homage to the ancestors, the gods, and the spirits of the land. The festival, spanning several days, culminates in a grand durbar—a gathering of chiefs, priests, and the community—to honor the spirits and seek their blessings for the coming year.

The durbar features colorful displays of traditional regalia, vibrant cultural performances, and the pouring of libations. The symbolic rituals are accompanied by traditional drumming and dancing, creating a festive atmosphere that resonates throughout Cape Coast. Fetu Afahye is not only a time of spiritual reflection but also a celebration of the resilience and cultural heritage of the Cape Coast people.

Asafotufiam: Commemorating Victories with the Ada People

The Asafotufiam Festival, celebrated by the Ada people, is a spirited commemoration of historical victories and a showcase of military prowess. The festival, which translates to "the firing of muskets," pays tribute to the bravery of the Ada warriors who defended their land against external threats.

Asafotufiam is marked by colorful processions, the firing of muskets, and the display of traditional military regalia. The festival includes drumming and dancing, with various clans and age groups participating in the celebrations. The rhythmic beats of the drums and the vibrant hues of the regalia create a visual and auditory spectacle that captures the spirit of the Ada people and their commitment to preserving their cultural legacy.

Chale Wote Street Art Festival: Nurturing Contemporary Creativity

In the heart of Accra, the Chale Wote Street Art Festival has emerged as a dynamic celebration of contemporary creativity, artistic expression, and cultural diversity. The festival, which started in 2011, transforms the streets of Jamestown into a vibrant canvas for visual arts, music, dance, and performance.

Chale Wote brings together local and international artists, musicians, and performers, creating a platform for the exchange of ideas and the celebration of diverse artistic expressions. The festival includes mural painting, street performances, art installations, and interactive exhibits. Chale Wote is a testament to the evolving cultural landscape of Ghana, where traditional and contemporary forms of creativity converge in a celebration of artistic freedom and cultural vibrancy.

Conclusion: A Symphony of Traditions

As we conclude our exploration of Ghanaian festivals and celebrations, we find ourselves immersed in a symphony of traditions that resonate across the diverse landscapes of the nation. Each festival is a unique melody, harmonizing history, spirituality, and the pulse of community life. The rhythmic beats of the drums, the vibrant colors of traditional regalia, and the communal joy expressed through dance and song create a cultural tapestry that transcends time.

Ghana's festivals serve as living testimonials to the resilience, creativity, and communal spirit of its people. They are not merely events on a calendar but living expressions of identity and shared heritage. Whether celebrating the harvest, commemorating historical victories, or fostering artistic expression, each festival contributes to the vibrant mosaic that defines Ghana's cultural landscape.

In the dance of the Adowa, the firing of muskets at Aboakyer, the rhythmic beats of the drums at Fetu Afahye, and the colorful street art of Chale Wote, we witness the soul of a nation pulsating with cultural richness. Ghanaian festivals are not only a reflection of the past but a bridge to the future, inviting both locals and visitors to partake in the symphony of traditions that make this West African nation an enchanting and dynamic destination.

Chapter 10
Ghana's Artistic Tapestry

In the intricate threads of Ghana's cultural fabric, the realm of art stands as a mesmerizing tapestry, woven with the threads of tradition, innovation, and a rich heritage that spans centuries. As we navigate this chapter, envision the canvas unfolding before you—a canvas adorned with vibrant hues, intricate patterns, and stories etched in every stroke. This is Ghana's artistic tapestry, a dynamic and evolving expression that mirrors the soul of a nation.

Traditional Art and Crafts:

Ghana's artistic journey commences with the traditional crafts that have been passed down through generations. From the Ashanti region's Kente cloth, characterized by its brilliant colors and intricate geometric designs, to the delicate Adinkra symbols stamped onto fabric, each piece tells a story deeply rooted in cultural symbolism. The skillful artistry of woodcarving, seen in the form of stools, masks, and figurines, is a testament to the mastery of Ghanaian artisans in transforming raw materials into pieces of cultural significance.

The bustling markets, such as Kumasi's Kejetia Market and Accra's Makola Market, serve as vibrant hubs where traditional crafts find new homes. The air is infused with the scent of fresh textiles, the hum of negotiations, and the visual spectacle of artisans at work, showcasing a living tradition that remains central to Ghana's cultural identity.

Contemporary Visual Arts:

Ghana's artistic landscape extends far beyond the traditional, embracing contemporary visual arts that reflect the nation's evolving narrative. In urban galleries and open-air spaces, a new generation of Ghanaian artists explores themes of identity, globalization, and societal change. Accra, in particular, has become a hotspot for contemporary art, with

EXPLORING GHANA

galleries like Nubuke Foundation and Nkrumah Volta Gallery fostering a space for innovative expressions.

The works of contemporary artists like El Anatsui, whose metal sculptures have gained international acclaim, bridge the gap between tradition and modernity. Through mediums such as painting, sculpture, and multimedia installations, artists in Ghana engage with global dialogues while staying rooted in their cultural context. The art becomes a mirror reflecting the complexities of the modern Ghanaian experience, inviting viewers to contemplate the intersections of history, identity, and progress.

Artisan Workshops and Craft Villages:

To truly appreciate Ghana's artistic prowess, one must venture into the heart of artisan workshops and craft villages scattered across the nation. These are sanctuaries where the rhythmic sounds of carving, weaving, and painting create a symphony of creativity. Ntonso, renowned for its Adinkra cloth, offers a glimpse into the meticulous stamping process where symbols convey messages of wisdom, proverbs, and cultural philosophy.

In the central region, Ahwiaa stands as a woodcarving haven, where artisans chisel away at mahogany and ebony to breathe life into ancestral motifs. Visiting these workshops is not just an observation of skill; it is an immersion into the intimate relationship between the artisan and their craft—a relationship that transcends the physical manifestation of the artwork.

Street Art and Murals:

The urban landscape of Accra and other cities serves as an expansive canvas for street artists, who use public spaces to communicate narratives, challenge perceptions, and contribute to social discourse. Street art in Ghana is a dynamic form of expression, addressing issues such as environmental conservation, social justice, and cultural pride.

The vibrant murals adorning city walls narrate stories of resilience, diversity, and unity. Jamestown in Accra has become a hotbed for street art, with its historic structures becoming a canvas for artists like Mohammed Awudu, whose murals celebrate the spirit of the community. These outdoor galleries breathe life into public spaces, transforming mundane walls into platforms for dialogue and reflection.

Ghana's Art Festivals:

Ghana's commitment to fostering artistic expression is exemplified through its vibrant art festivals. The Chale Wote Street Art Festival, held annually in Accra, transforms the city into a kaleidoscope of creativity. Artists, both local and international, converge to showcase installations, performances, and exhibitions that transcend conventional gallery spaces.

Similarly, the Nkabom Literary Art Festival celebrates the intersection of literature and visual arts. Through poetry slams, storytelling sessions, and art installations, the festival becomes a melting pot of artistic disciplines, emphasizing the interconnectedness of various creative expressions in Ghana.

Preservation of Artistic Traditions:

While Ghana embraces contemporary artistic expressions, there is a concerted effort to preserve traditional craftsmanship. Organizations like the Ghana Museums and Monuments Board play a pivotal role in safeguarding cultural heritage. Museums, such as the National Museum in Accra, house collections that span from ancient artifacts to contemporary art, providing a comprehensive view of Ghana's artistic evolution.

Artisan cooperatives and NGOs, such as the Craft Village in Tamale and the Art Centre in Kumasi, work tirelessly to empower local artisans, ensuring the continuity of traditional practices. These initiatives not only contribute to the economic sustainability of artisans but also serve as bastions for the transmission of artistic knowledge to future generations.

Art as Cultural Diplomacy:

Ghana's art has transcended national borders, becoming a form of cultural diplomacy that fosters international dialogue and understanding. Initiatives like the Ghana UK-based African Art Gallery (GUBA)

Awards recognize and celebrate the contributions of Ghanaian artists in the global arena. Through these platforms, Ghana's artistic narrative resonates on an international stage, fostering connections and dispelling cultural misconceptions.

Ghanaian embassies and cultural centers abroad often feature exhibitions and events that showcase the nation's artistic wealth. These endeavors serve not only to share Ghana's cultural vibrancy but also to engage in cross-cultural conversations that transcend geographical boundaries.

Art and Cultural Identity:

At its core, Ghana's artistic tapestry is inseparable from its cultural identity. Whether through traditional symbols woven into textiles, contemporary installations challenging societal norms, or the vibrant hues of street art adorning city walls, art becomes a reflection of Ghana's multifaceted identity.

Artistic expressions in Ghana are not confined to galleries; they spill into daily life, influencing fashion, interior design, and public spaces. The ubiquitous presence of art reinforces its role as a dynamic and integral part of the nation's collective consciousness. In the faces of sculpted masks, the rhythmic beats of traditional dance, and the bold strokes of contemporary paintings, Ghanaians find a mirror that reflects the depth and diversity of their cultural heritage.

Art as a Catalyst for Change:

Beyond aesthetics, Ghana's art has the power to effect social change. Artists and cultural activists utilize their platforms to address pressing issues, amplify marginalized voices, and challenge societal norms. The art becomes a conduit for conversations about gender, politics, and environmental sustainability.

Through the lens of photographers like James Barnor, Ghana's social history unfolds, capturing moments of transition and resilience. The art, in its myriad forms, becomes a catalyst for dialogue, prompting viewers to question, reflect, and engage with the complexities of the world around them.

The Future of Ghana's Artistic Landscape:
As we conclude our exploration of Ghana's artistic tapestry, it is essential to ponder the trajectory of the nation's creative landscape. The future holds the promise of continued innovation, collaboration, and the nurturing of emerging talents. Initiatives supporting art education, such as the Nubuke Foundation's mentorship programs, contribute to the cultivation of the next generation of artists.

Technology, too, plays a role in shaping Ghana's artistic future. Digital platforms provide artists with global visibility, enabling them to connect with diverse audiences and participate in global conversations. Virtual galleries and online exhibitions extend the reach of Ghanaian art beyond physical borders, contributing to the democratization of artistic appreciation.

In this chapter, we have traversed the expansive terrain of Ghana's artistic expression—from the ancient traditions embedded in crafts to the contemporary visual language that graces urban spaces. The artistic tapestry of Ghana is not static; it is a living, breathing entity that continues to evolve, influenced by tradition, propelled by innovation, and imbued with the spirit of a nation that embraces the beauty of its cultural mosaic.

As you navigate the vibrant markets, explore artisan workshops, and engage with contemporary galleries, may you feel the pulse of Ghana's artistic heartbeat. Let the colors, shapes, and narratives encountered in these pages serve as an invitation to delve deeper, to engage with the art not merely as an observer but as a participant in the ongoing story of Ghana's creative evolution. The canvas is vast, the palette diverse—welcome to Ghana's artistic tapestry, where every stroke tells a story, and every creation is a celebration of cultural richness.

Chapter 11
Coastal Charms - Exploring Ghana's Hidden Beaches

Ghana, a nation known for its historical landmarks, cultural vibrancy, and lush landscapes, is also blessed with a coastline that unfolds like a well-guarded secret. As we delve into this chapter, envision the rhythmic cadence of the Gulf of Guinea, the soft embrace of golden sands, and the untold stories whispered by the ocean breeze. This is the lesser-explored realm of Ghana's hidden beaches—a coastal treasure trove waiting to be discovered.

Busua Beach: The Secluded Haven
Nestled on the western coast of Ghana, Busua Beach emerges as a haven of tranquility. Far from the bustling urban centers, Busua offers a serene escape where time seems to slow down. The beach, flanked by coconut palms and fishing boats, invites visitors to unwind on its powdery sands.

As the Atlantic waves gently caress the shore, Busua becomes a canvas for relaxation. The beach's secluded charm is amplified by the absence of large crowds, allowing visitors to savor the beauty of the coastline in solitude. Whether it's a leisurely stroll along the water's edge or an afternoon spent watching the sun dip below the horizon, Busua captivates with its simplicity and natural allure.

Ada Foah: Where River Meets Sea
In the southeastern corner of Ghana, at the confluence of the Volta River and the Atlantic Ocean, lies the enchanting town of Ada Foah. This coastal paradise offers a unique blend of riverine and seaside landscapes, creating an idyllic setting for those seeking a diverse coastal experience.

The Volta Estuary, with its meandering channels and lush mangrove forests, adds a distinctive charm to Ada Foah. Visitors can embark on boat cruises along the estuary, exploring the intricate network of waterways and encountering vibrant birdlife. The journey culminates as the river seamlessly merges with the ocean, creating a picturesque tableau where the elements harmonize in perfect equilibrium.

Kokrobite Beach: Bohemian Vibes by the Sea

For those drawn to the bohemian spirit, Kokrobite Beach beckons with its laid-back ambiance and artistic flair. Located just a short drive from Accra, Kokrobite is a magnet for travelers seeking a beach experience infused with creativity and community.

This stretch of coastline has evolved into a cultural hub, hosting drumming circles, art workshops, and live music events. The vibrant colors of beachfront murals, the rhythmic beats of traditional drumming, and the scent of grilled seafood create an atmosphere that transcends the ordinary. Kokrobite's beaches are not just landscapes; they are stages for cultural expression and communal celebration.

Cape Three Points: Where Land Meets Sea

At the southwestern tip of Ghana lies Cape Three Points, a destination that holds the distinction of being the country's southernmost point. This remote and pristine location offers an unspoiled coastal retreat, where the vast expanse of the Atlantic unfolds panoramically.

Cape Three Points is a destination for the intrepid traveler, accessible by a scenic trek through lush tropical forests. The reward for this journey is the sight of the Cape's iconic lighthouse perched atop rugged cliffs, providing a breathtaking vantage point to witness the meeting of land and sea. The beaches surrounding the cape are secluded and pristine, inviting visitors to revel in the untouched beauty of Ghana's southern coastline.

Anomabu and Cape Coast: Historical Beaches

As we explore Ghana's hidden beaches, it is essential to pay homage to the historical significance embedded in the sands of Anomabu and Cape Coast. These coastal towns, marked by the haunting presence of forts and castles, also boast stretches of shoreline that resonate with the echoes of a complex past.

Anomabu Beach, with its palm-fringed shores, stands as a poignant reminder of the transatlantic slave trade. The beachfront, flanked by Fort William and Fort Sebastian, invites contemplation as the waves narrate stories of resilience and remembrance. Cape Coast, home to Cape Coast Castle, combines historical reflection with coastal beauty. The castle, perched on the edge of the sea, serves as a portal to Ghana's past, while the adjacent beach offers a serene escape where history and nature converge.

Axim: Gold Coast's Hidden Gem

On the westernmost edge of Ghana lies Axim, a coastal town that was once a pivotal hub in the Gold Coast's history. Axim's beaches, relatively undiscovered by mass tourism, exude an untouched charm that captures the essence of a bygone era.

The Axim Beach Resort, nestled along the shoreline, offers a retreat into luxury amid the coastal tranquility. Visitors can explore the remnants of Fort St. Anthony, an ancient Portuguese fort that stands sentinel over the sea. Axim's beaches, fringed by coconut palms and dotted with fishing canoes, provide a serene escape for those seeking solitude and a connection to Ghana's maritime legacy.

Beyond the Waves: Water Activities and Marine Life

Ghana's hidden beaches are not only about basking in the sun and absorbing the coastal scenery; they also offer a playground for water enthusiasts. Snorkeling, kayaking, and paddleboarding become avenues to explore the underwater wonders along the coastline.

The marine life off Ghana's shores adds another layer of allure to its hidden beaches. Turtle nesting sites, particularly along the beaches of Ada Foah, become sanctuaries for these ancient travelers. Conservation efforts in collaboration with local communities aim to protect these nesting grounds, allowing visitors a rare opportunity to witness the delicate dance between turtles and the sea.

Community Engagement and Sustainable Tourism:

As we venture into the hidden beaches of Ghana, it is crucial to approach this exploration with a mindset of sustainable tourism and community engagement. Many of these coastal communities, while eager to share their natural treasures, also face the challenges of preserving their environments and cultural heritage.

Initiatives that promote responsible tourism, such as beach cleanups, conservation awareness programs, and collaborations with local communities, contribute to the preservation of Ghana's hidden coastal gems. Engaging with local guides, supporting community-led initiatives, and respecting the natural environment ensure that these beaches remain pristine for generations to come.

Sunset Serenades and Night Skies:

The allure of Ghana's hidden beaches extends beyond daylight hours. As the sun begins its descent, the beaches become stages for breathtaking sunset serenades. The horizon transforms into a canvas of warm hues, casting a golden glow over the sands and the sea. Sunset at these hidden beaches is not merely a celestial event; it is a symphony of colors that encapsulates the beauty of the coastal landscape.

As night falls, the beaches offer a different kind of enchantment. Far from the urban lights, the night skies become a celestial spectacle. Stargazing on these remote shores reveals a tapestry of constellations, providing a serene and awe-inspiring conclusion to a day of coastal exploration.

Conclusion: Coastal Odyssey in Ghana's Hidden Gems

In the final strokes of this chapter, as we bid adieu to the hidden beaches of Ghana, let the echoes of the waves and the imprints in the sand linger in your imagination. The coastal odyssey through Busua, Ada Foah, Kokrobite, Cape Three Points, Anomabu, Cape Coast, Axim, and beyond is an invitation to unravel the secrets of Ghana's shoreline.

May these hidden beaches become not just destinations but experiences etched in memory—an immersion into the natural wonders and cultural richness of Ghana's coastal splendor. Whether seeking solitude on secluded shores, engaging in water activities, or embracing the historical narratives embedded in the sands, Ghana's hidden beaches beckon as a coastal odyssey waiting to be explored.

Chapter 12
Practical Travel Tips

Embarking on a journey to Ghana, with its rich cultural tapestry, diverse landscapes, and warm hospitality, requires thoughtful preparation and an understanding of the practicalities that enhance the travel experience. Whether navigating urban centers, exploring historical sites, or immersing oneself in the vibrant local culture, a combination of practical knowledge and cultural awareness contributes to a seamless and enriching journey. In this chapter, we provide a comprehensive guide to practical travel tips for navigating the intricacies of Ghana, ensuring that every traveler can make the most of their time in this captivating West African nation.

1. Visa and Entry Requirements

Before setting foot on Ghanaian soil, it is crucial to check the visa and entry requirements. Most travelers to Ghana require a visa, which can be obtained from Ghanaian embassies or consulates. It is advisable to start the visa application process well in advance of the planned travel date to ensure a smooth and timely approval.

Additionally, travelers should check the validity of their passports, which should have at least six months remaining before expiration. Entry requirements may vary, so staying informed about any changes or updates to visa regulations is essential for a hassle-free entry into Ghana.

2. Health and Vaccinations

Ensuring good health is a priority for any traveler, and preparing for a trip to Ghana involves taking certain health precautions. Vaccinations for yellow fever are mandatory for entry into Ghana, and a yellow fever vaccination certificate is required. It is advisable to consult with a healthcare professional or travel clinic well in advance to receive necessary vaccinations and medical advice based on the specific travel itinerary.

Malaria is prevalent in certain regions of Ghana, and prophylactic medication is recommended. Travelers should also carry a basic medical kit, including essential medications, insect repellent, and any prescription medicines they may need during their stay. Hydration is crucial in the tropical climate, so carrying a reusable water bottle and staying well-hydrated is essential.

3. Currency and Banking

The official currency of Ghana is the Ghanaian Cedi (GHS). While credit cards are accepted in urban centers and major establishments, it is advisable to carry some local currency for transactions in smaller shops, markets, and rural areas. ATMs are widely available in cities, and cash withdrawals can be made using international credit or debit cards. Informing banks about travel plans helps prevent any issues with card transactions abroad.

Travelers should be cautious when using ATMs and prefer those located in well-lit, secure areas. It's recommended to carry some cash in smaller denominations for purchases in markets and for tips.

4. Language and Communication

English is the official language of Ghana, making communication relatively straightforward for English-speaking travelers. However, Ghanaians often speak local languages such as Twi, Ga, Fante, and Ewe. Learning a few basic phrases in these languages can enhance the travel experience and facilitate interactions with local communities.

While urban areas and tourist destinations generally have reliable mobile network coverage, remote areas may have limited connectivity. Purchasing a local SIM card upon arrival can provide cost-effective communication options. Apps with offline maps and translation features can be useful for navigating unfamiliar areas.

5. Transportation

Ghana's transportation infrastructure caters to various modes of travel, offering options for both urban and intercity journeys.

- **Taxis and Ride-Sharing:** Taxis are readily available in urban areas, and ride-sharing services operate in major cities. It's

advisable to agree on fares before starting the journey, as taxis may not always use meters.
- **Tro-Tros:** Tro-Tros are shared minibusses or vans that serve as a common mode of transportation for short to medium distances. They operate on fixed routes, and fares are often negotiable.
- **Intercity Buses:** For longer journeys between cities, intercity buses provide a comfortable and reliable means of transportation. Several reputable bus companies operate scheduled services.
- **Domestic Flights:** Domestic flights are available for those looking to cover long distances quickly. Local airlines offer regular flights between major cities and regions.
- **Renting a Car:** Renting a car provides flexibility for exploring remote areas. However, road conditions may vary, and it's essential to adhere to traffic regulations.

6. Accommodation

Ghana offers a range of accommodation options, from luxury hotels to budget-friendly guesthouses. Booking accommodation in advance is advisable, especially during peak tourist seasons. Major cities and tourist destinations have a variety of lodging choices, but availability may be limited in more remote areas.

When selecting accommodation, factors such as location, amenities, and reviews can guide the decision-making process. It's beneficial to consider options that align with the travel itinerary and preferences.

7. Safety and Security

Ghana is generally considered safe for travelers, and the country has a reputation for hospitality. However, like any travel destination, it's important to remain vigilant and take precautions:

- **Local Advice:** Seeking advice from locals or accommodation

staff about safe areas, potential risks, and recommended practices is valuable.
- **Valuables:** Keeping valuables secure and avoiding conspicuous displays of wealth helps deter opportunistic crime.
- **Health Precautions:** Taking precautions against mosquito bites, staying hydrated, and following food safety practices contribute to overall well-being.

8. Cultural Etiquette and Respect

Respecting local customs and cultural norms is integral to a positive travel experience in Ghana. Greetings are an essential part of Ghanaian culture, and a simple "hello" or "good morning" goes a long way in establishing rapport. It's customary to ask for permission before taking photographs, especially in rural areas or at cultural events.

Dressing modestly is appreciated, particularly when visiting religious or traditional sites. Removing shoes before entering someone's home is a common practice, and it's polite to accept or offer items with the right hand.

9. Weather and Packing

Ghana's climate is tropical, characterized by two main seasons: the wet season and the dry season. The wet season typically runs from April to October, with heavy rainfall. The dry season, from November to March, features hot temperatures and lower humidity.

Packing considerations include:

- Lightweight and breathable clothing suitable for warm weather.
- Rain gear and a travel umbrella for the wet season.
- Comfortable walking shoes for exploring diverse landscapes.
- Sunscreen, insect repellent, and a basic first aid kit.
- Adapters for electrical outlets, as Ghana uses the British-style Type G socket.

10. Respect for Local Customs and Traditions

Cultural sensitivity is key to fostering positive interactions with local communities. Learning about and respecting local customs, traditions, and social norms demonstrates appreciation for Ghana's rich cultural heritage. Observing and participating in local customs, such as traditional dances or festivals, enhances the travel experience and promotes cultural exchange.

In conclusion, Ghana beckons travelers with its cultural richness, natural beauty, and warm hospitality. By embracing practical travel tips and cultural awareness, visitors can immerse themselves in the diverse tapestry of Ghana, forging memorable experiences and contributing to the sustainable and responsible exploration of this enchanting West African nation.

Epilogue
A Journey Unveiled

As we conclude our expedition through the vibrant landscapes, rich cultures, and warm-hearted communities of Ghana, the echoes of this West African odyssey linger in the recesses of our memories. Ghana, a nation adorned with the hues of history, tradition, and resilience, has unfolded before our eyes as a tapestry of experiences, each thread woven with care by the hands of time.

From the bustling markets of Accra to the serene shores of Lake Volta, and from the ancient forts of Cape Coast to the lively streets of Kumasi, Ghana has revealed itself as a treasure trove of diversity. Its people, the custodians of ancestral legacies, have welcomed us with open hearts, inviting us to share in their stories, partake in their traditions, and dance to the rhythms of life.

In the pages of this travel guide, we embarked on a journey that transcended the physical boundaries of geography. We explored the cultural mosaic of festivals that pulse through the nation, resonating with the beats of drums, the fervor of dance, and the spirit of communal celebration. We navigated the culinary landscape, savoring the flavors of jollof rice, banku and tilapia, and the sweetness of plantain chips, discovering that Ghanaian cuisine is not just a culinary adventure but a profound connection to the land and its people.

Our sojourn through historical sites, such as the Cape Coast Castle and Elmina Castle, unearthed the layers of Ghana's past, where the shadows of transatlantic slavery met the resilience of the human spirit. In Kumasi, the cultural hub, we witnessed the living legacy of the Asante kingdom, a testament to the harmonious coexistence of tradition and modernity.

The wild wonders of Mole National Park and the adventurous canopy walk at Kakum National Park reminded us of Ghana's commitment to conservation and the intrinsic link between its people and the natural world. The tranquil beauty of the Volta Region, with its serene lakes and lush landscapes, offered a retreat into the heart of nature.

Beyond borders, we explored the interconnected tapestry of West Africa, venturing into Togo and Côte d'Ivoire, where each nation revealed its unique character while contributing to the collective identity of the region.

In this epilogue, as we reflect on the journey, we are reminded that travel is not merely a physical movement from one place to another. It is a profound exploration of the self, a cultural exchange that leaves indelible imprints on our perspectives and a testament to the shared humanity that binds us all.

Ghana, with its open arms and vibrant spirit, has left an indelible mark on our hearts. The call of the Adowa drums, the laughter of children playing in the streets, and the whispers of the Atlantic breeze at Cape Coast—all these moments coalesce into a symphony of memories that transcend time.

As we bid farewell to this enchanting corner of the African continent, may the echoes of our footsteps through the markets, the rhythms of the festivals, and the taste of Ghanaian cuisine linger, serving as a perpetual reminder of the beauty that resides in the unity of diversity.

Ghana, with its radiant smiles and kaleidoscope of cultures, has shared its essence with us—a gift that transcends the confines of a travel guide and invites us to become storytellers of our own West African adventure. Until our paths cross again, whether in the vibrant streets of Accra or the serene landscapes of the Volta Region, may the spirit of Ghana accompany us on our continued journey through the vast tapestry of our world.

Appendix
Additional Resources

As you embark on your journey through Ghana, consider these additional resources to enhance your exploration, deepen your understanding, and make the most of your travel experience:

1. **Online Travel Communities:**
   - Connect with fellow travelers and glean insights from their experiences on platforms such as TripAdvisor, Lonely Planet's Thorn Tree Forum, and Reddit's travel subreddits.
2. **Language Learning Apps:**
   - Familiarize yourself with basic phrases in local languages using language learning apps like Duolingo or Babbel. While English is widely spoken, learning a few words in Twi, Ga, Fante, or Ewe can enrich your interactions.
3. **Local Newspapers and Magazines:**
   - Stay updated on local events, festivals, and current affairs by exploring Ghanaian newspapers and magazines. Some notable publications include "The Ghanaian Times," "Daily Graphic," and "New African Magazine."
4. **Local Tour Operators:**
   - Enhance your travel experience by engaging with reputable local tour operators. They can provide customized itineraries, guided tours, and insights into off-the-beaten-path destinations.
5. **Literature and Films:**
   - Immerse yourself in Ghanaian literature and films to

gain cultural insights. Explore works by authors like Ayi Kwei Armah ("The Beautyful Ones Are Not Yet Born") and films such as "Heritage Africa" and "Sankofa."

6. **Government Tourism Websites:**
    - Visit official tourism websites for up-to-date information on attractions, events, and travel regulations. The Ghana Tourism Authority's website is a valuable resource for planning your trip.

7. **Photography Exhibitions:**
    - Experience the visual allure of Ghana through photography exhibitions. Check local galleries, museums, or online platforms for exhibits that showcase the country's landscapes, people, and culture.

8. **Educational Workshops and Events:**
    - Attend workshops or cultural events organized by local institutions and NGOs. These events provide opportunities for immersive learning and interaction with the local community.

9. **Embassies and Consulates:**
    - Contact the Ghanaian embassy or consulate in your home country for additional travel information, visa assistance, and updates on any travel advisories.

10. **Online Cultural Courses:**
    - Enroll in online courses or webinars that delve into Ghanaian history, art, and culture. Platforms like Coursera or Udemy often offer courses created by experts in the field.

Remember that travel is a dynamic experience, and these resources can serve as valuable companions to your guidebook, offering diverse perspectives and enriching your exploration of Ghana. Safe travels!

Milton Keynes UK
Ingram Content Group UK Ltd.
UKHW010420131223
434231UK00001B/100